# From the Source:
# An Introduction to Channeling

# From the Source:
# An Introduction to Channeling

## Jack Armstrong
Author of *Lessons from the Source*

Wisdom from the Source Publications

*For Jessie, with enormous gratitude.*

*This form of communication, which you allow to flow at many different times and in many circumstances, is an energetic vibration that is flowing from the one consciousness to that same consciousness, personified as you, and then will be shared and re-transmitted in one form or another with other individual expressions of that same consciousness, and it will touch each in different ways that are appropriate to their own needs.*

Transcribed April 26, 2008

# CONTENTS

# Introduction

Ever since I published *Lessons from the Source* in 2008, people have been asking me about myself and about this process of channeling wisdom from another dimension – how it started, what happens, how I know it's the real deal.

This book is intended to answer some of those questions – and to encourage you to think about your own connection to Source and ways in which it might express through you. I'll tell you about my own experience with Inner Dictation and describe the process as best I can, include some observations about it from Source, and give you some practical suggestions about how you might try to explore it on your own.

Even after decades of experiencing this form of communication, I continue to be in awe of it. I don't know why I was chosen to be the recipient of these teachings, but I've gladly accepted that role and still enjoy playing it.

In thinking about how best to share this phenomenon with you, I've gone back through the massive amounts of material I've received and transcribed over the years and have found some wonderful passages from Source about the process that offer a much more enlightening perspective than I would be able to come up with from my conscious human mind.

One day in August, 2008, I wrote down these words which almost seem to have been preparing me for telling this story:

> *Simplicity must be central to your telling of the story. You are a channel through which truth is being presented in a way that will resonate with those who need it. Compared with other, equally valid and important expressions of the one truth, the interpretation you are sharing is simple and direct. So should be the way you convey it. A brief, simple explanation and introduction will be all that will be required for those for whom it is intended. As you have understood and expressed so frequently, this is not about you. You have been given a gift, and you are sharing it with others.*
>
> *You have just felt a comparison with the sharing of the loaves and fishes, and it is appropriate. And no, this is not a comparison of you with the Master in a way that is intended to prove yourself. Neither was that the case with Jesus. The multitudes were hungry for nourishment, and he was given a gift that appeared small and insignificant, and he took it and blessed it and saw it bringing nourishment, and he shared it*

*with those who needed it and would benefit from it. The small amount of food seemed insignificant, yet someone gave it to the Master, trusting that a blessing would occur, and he in turn shared it in a way that fed the hunger of others. He did not do so in a way that would be self-serving or self-aggrandizing. He simply understood that he could share the gift, and he did so without reservation, trusting that the need would be met. It was a simple act, carried out with love and complete trust.*

And so, with love and complete trust, I will share with you my experiences, my thoughts about them, and some much grander observations about this phenomenon from Source itself.

Jack Armstrong

# My Own Experience with Inner Dictation

As I explained in *Lessons from the Source*, the form of channeling I've been experiencing for more than 35 years is called Inner Dictation. Simply learning that there was a name for it was very gratifying, as was finding out that people have been experiencing it for centuries – and that *A Course in Miracles* is perhaps the most well-known example.

Over the years I've become very comfortable with this phenomenon and my role in it, but that wasn't always the case, and it seems appropriate to begin by giving you some information about how I first experienced it and how it has evolved since then.

## How the Process Began: The First Communication

I lived in Southern California for a year in the early 1970s and during that time met a woman who had lived there all her life, whom I later married and with whom I spent more than three decades together. She introduced me to the Lake Shrine, a beautiful, peaceful setting near the ocean that was founded and dedicated by Paramahansa Yoganada and still is run by the Self Realization Fellowship. There is a small lake, waterfalls, a meditation chapel and a beautifully landscaped path through a garden-like setting.

From my very first visit, I was captivated by the tranquility and powerful energy of that place and its honoring of the world's five principal religious belief systems, and I went back from time to time simply to be quiet and meditate and experience the peacefulness.

Although we moved away from California and lived elsewhere for eleven years, we would go back at least once a year to visit family and celebrate holidays, and I usually would make time available to get away by myself and visit the Lake Shrine.

One day in December, 1978, I got there and felt moved to take a pen and a notebook in with me. I wasn't clear why – it just felt right.

When the writing started happening for the first time, there was no dramatic moment, no flash of insight. I simply started writing. Thoughts – sentences, actually – were coming to my mind, and I wrote them down like a scribe. I didn't know why I was doing it or what was happening, but I allowed it to happen.

There was never an audible voice that I "heard." Just thoughts, in the form of sentences. While almost all the communications I've received since then have come in the first person singular ("I") and have been directed to me ("you"), on that first occasion they were in the first person plural ("we").

Over the decades that I've been having this experience, the material that comes through often is lengthy and complex, holds together beautifully, and flows effortlessly from one topic to another. That first time, however, it came in a series of sentences or brief paragraphs that felt random and disconnected, but that in retrospect seem to have been addressing two basic topics: living in joy and being open to guidance.

The very first words I wrote down were:

*What is it you are seeking? You must define the limits of your desires before they can be realized. Live to manifest joy and happiness. Calm down and manifest joy. Get in rhythm with the Cosmos, and the answers will be there.*

Earlier that year, I had begun a new job and within a few months had become so stressed about it that I ended up hospitalized with a bleeding ulcer. Clearly the absence of joy was a big issue for me, so I guess it's not coincidental that that was a topic from the get-go.

Here are most of the other sentences that came through, in the order they were written:

*Wipe away the shell – the static – around you. You're not letting us in. We want to help. The answers are easy. The future is good.*

*Concentrate on what we are saying and you'll hear us. Free your mind and body. Open the door to your soul.*

*Do you see the beauty around you? Your soul is more beautiful and purer than any of this. You are a child of God, who is always with you. His hand is always there ready to comfort you and show you the way, but the fog you have created around you keeps you from seeing it.*

*You're afraid to hear what we say. When this happens, the truth will not come through. Open all of your channels and allow the truth to flow in through every pore.*

*You want to know where to direct your life next. You are not directing it, though you have free choice to refuse the obvious.*

*Still we speak to you of joy, but you are enshrouded by sadness. Do not fret and fuss. Listen with all of your senses to the music of the spheres and allow joy to enter your life. You are part of life. You are in control, if you will but attune yourself to the truth.*

*Keep a halo around your head, and a white light around your whole body. You are in the midst of a joyous manifestation. You will grow through expressing joy and opening your channels to the truth.*

*The answers you are seeking will be made clear to you if you will but relax and make yourself available to the answers.*

*Express love, be happy, enjoy your family, have faith, be patient, know that you are in the midst of the stream of life.*

*Do not despair of specific decisions until you have placed yourself in the stream of power and truth again. Then will answers be clear.*

*Enjoyment is the key, and it is so easy. It's a natural life process, but you sometimes make it so difficult. You must just believe that what is happening to you is real.*

It's interesting to me now, as I look back at those words for the first time in many years, to realize that I clearly was being introduced to this form of communication. In several different ways, "they" were saying that it always was available if I could just let go of the "fog" or "static" around me and then free my mind and body, open the door to my soul, and "allow the truth to flow in through every pore."

Sometimes I'm rather dense, but I honestly didn't have a clue at that time what this was all about. I had never heard about this type of channeling, and phrases like "get in rhythm with the Cosmos" or "the music of the spheres" or "the stream of life" were entirely new to me.

I don't remember if I shared that experience with my wife or not, but I probably did. In any event, I put the writing aside and essentially forgot about it.

## How the Process Began: The Second Communication

The next time I experienced this phenomenon was two years later, on January 2, 1981, also at the Lake Shrine. My guess is that I went back there to see if something similar might happen again. As before, the sentences seemed random, but joy was still a primary topic. Interestingly, though, the voice had changed to the first person singular, and the statements seemed to start addressing some of the topics that would become consistent over the years. Here are some of the things I wrote down:

*Love is the key. Know that I am God, that you are God, and that we all are God and act accordingly.*

*The answers for your future are all around you. To understand them, you must lighten the load you have placed on your own shoulders, see this life for what it is, and know that we all are God.*

*You are so concerned about the future. Relax and enjoy this moment. It is the essence of all existence. To understand life, it is necessary to understand yourself.*

*All of these concerns about the physical world are meaningless. A job, a home, money – these are mere trappings of your true existence.*

*You are not isolated. You are one with all people and all things. Your existence is their existence, and theirs is yours. You see the absolute purity of that flower. You are just as pure. All beings should express joy in their own existence. Flowers come and go, but during their time on this plane they radiate joy and beauty. You should do the same. Live to bring joy to others. Live to realize your beauty as a child of God.*

*Joy is so difficult for you. It must become as much a part of your life as breathing. When you wake in the morning, give thanks to God with joy in your heart. Live with joy at your side and in your heart every minute.*

*You ask how to achieve joy, yet it is already so much a part of you. Let it become part of your aura.*

*When you are able to make joy and love an integral part of your life, the woes that you have selected for yourself on this plane are easily manageable. Lighten your heart. Be at peace.*

## How the Process Evolved

The third experience was nearly another two years later, in October of 1982. But after that the communications began to come in clusters: at least one (and as many as nine) each year between 1983 and the last three months of 1995, when the material in *Lessons from the Source* was transcribed – 42 times over a period of almost 13 years.

I must have known all of this was important, because I held onto the writings and eventually typed them all up, but I still didn't know what was happening or why. One of the things I was guided to do was to write the date at the top of the first page of each of the communications. With very few exceptions I've done that, and the dates have allowed me to arrange almost all of the writings in chronological order.

In looking back at the dates on which I did the writing during that 13-year period, it's clear that I often made the decision to sit down with pen and paper during times of significant stress in my life – almost always regarding issues related to my work. Sometimes the words were written on things like a napkin or the back of a store receipt, which would seem to indicate that I must have felt desperate for help and guidance and turned to the writings on the spur of the moment as the way to get them.

Beginning with that third communication in 1982, there was a noticeable change in the format and the tone of the writings. They were much more detailed, explored specific themes or topics, and came in longer paragraphs that followed each other logically. It suddenly began to feel like the "voice" was speaking to me as a friend or mentor. Someone once told me she felt that reading *Lessons from the Source* was like having a private, one-on-one coaching session with God, and that describes it beautifully. With very few exceptions, that tone has continued in the communications to this day.

The other big change, that has continued ever since, was that I began to be addressed as "John." That is my given name, but I've been called Jack from day one. I've removed all of the references to me by name in the materials I've shared with others, but it still is fascinating that I'm always John to the Source.

## How *Lessons from the Source* Was Born

If you've read *Lessons from the Source*, you know from the "Notes from the Author" Appendix that the material in the book was received during the last three months of 1995.

I had left a 20-year career in nonprofit management at the end of 1992 and redirected the course of my professional life completely. Things weren't working out as I had hoped, and those years were very challenging.

I felt cut adrift from my spiritual moorings and read a number of different spiritual books hoping to find guidance that would be helpful.

Late in September of 1995, I bought Julia Cameron's book, *The Artist's Way,* and found her concept of morning pages to be intriguing.

Morning pages were one of two tools she offered for what she called "creative recovery," and she described them by saying: "Put simply, the morning pages are three pages of longhand writing, strictly stream-of-consciousness." In other words, just get up every morning and write down whatever comes to you. That seemed like an interesting concept, so I decided to give it a try. It was September 28, 1995.

Before that day, it had been nearly seven months since the last time I had experienced my communication with Source, yet these were the first words that came through on September 28:

> *You want to communicate with me, but you seem not to know how. Have you forgotten this medium? How many times have I spoken directly to you in this way? Has it ever failed you? If meditation (which still is very important to your wholeness and integration) does not seem to offer you what you need, then discipline yourself to communicate in this way each day. The "morning pages" concept is a wonderful one for you. You are extraordinarily well attuned in this way.*

What is fascinating in retrospect is that it never occurred to me at the time that there might have been some similarity between writing the morning pages and the experiences I had been having over the years. It just seemed like something worth trying, but I'm certain now that I was guided to the morning pages idea in order to get me back on board with my writing and to give me a reason to engage in that communication on a more consistent basis.

Immediately after that "welcome back" introduction, the material that eventually would be included in *Lessons from the Source* began to flow. The very next paragraph I wrote was what ended up being the second excerpt included in the section titled *A Higher Perspective* on page 24 of *Lessons from the Source*. What you'll read there is, verbatim, the exact wording that came through to me next.

Between then and the end of the year, I kept my commitment to myself to write every day, and the outpouring of material was astonishing. It was during that time that the voice speaking through the writings began referring to them as "lessons," and the vast majority of what was written during those three months was eventually included in the book.

## A Few Other Things You Ought to Know About Me

After that three-month period, the writings became a regular part of my life. While this never again became a daily experience over such an extended period of time, I would have an inner knowing when it was time to sit down with my notebook and open myself to the communication, and that has continued to this day.

There are two rather embarrassing realities about this that I mentioned in the book, but will repeat here simply because they feel important to share with you.

The first is that, because I had no frame of reference for this type of channeling and had no idea why it was happening, I told almost no one outside of my immediate family about it. One of the messages I had been given while growing up (and that stuck with me for most of my life) was that what other people thought about me was very important, and that it was my responsibility to convey the best possible impression to them (whoever they might be).

Because of that, I clearly was not about to tell friends or family members that I was receiving and writing down messages from some unknown place or entity. I didn't understand it myself, and I certainly was not going to try to explain it to anyone else, so I kept it as my closely-guarded secret for decades.

(One of the many blessings from my decision to "come out of the closet" about all of this and publish *Lessons from the Source* was the number of people who contacted me to thank me for going public with my secret, because they had been having similar experiences for years and also were afraid to tell others about them.)

The other, even more embarrassing, thing I need to tell you is that I totally ignored these beautiful interpretations of spiritual truth that were being give to me regularly. I knew they were powerful and that they were intended (at least initially) to help me in my own spiritual growth and understanding, but as soon as I finished with a specific writing, I would close my notebook (sometimes without even reading back over what had come through) and put it into the nightstand beside my bed.

Over the years, the number of notebooks in the nightstand kept growing, and I was even moved periodically to type up the contents, but I flat out ignored the wisdom that was being shared with me.

Think about that – I continued to fret and worry and stress about all kinds of things in my life and to try to make things happen the way I thought they should. I kept up my spiritual seeking by reading spiritual books, taking classes and trying out new churches, but nothing ever seemed to stick. I understood the concepts intellectually but wasn't able to live them and put them into practice in my life.

And there I was, sitting on a treasure trove of beautiful and powerful spiritual teachings that I never even bothered to go back and read.

There is one other little sidebar that you ought to be aware of that probably played a factor in my inability to live what I was being taught – and that also might offer a hint as to why I was chosen to receive the teachings.

My mind doesn't remember concepts very well. Every day I find myself remembering names and dates and places and smells and song lyrics and all other kinds of seemingly insignificant little details from my life, but bigger concepts don't seem to stick.

If I were to go to a movie tonight and you asked me tomorrow what the plot was, I would have a hard time piecing it all back together. I'll read a spiritual book or novel, and the contents don't stay with me for long.

And when I'm doing the writing, I remember almost nothing about what has come through me – even from one sentence to the next. When a "session" (for lack of a better word) is over, the contents are pretty much gone from my conscious mind.

As you'll read later, one of the essential aspects of Inner Dictation is that the human mind has to let go of any questioning of the words or concepts that are being presented, and I'm guessing that my inability to remember what has come through might make me a more open channel to allow the process to happen.

# Two Descriptions of Inner Dictation

## How I Describe It

When people ask me about this form of channeling and what it's like to experience it, I usually say something like this:

It's all about getting my human mind out of the way and then trusting and allowing the communication to happen. I seldom have any advance notice about when it's going to be time to do the writing or any indication of what the subject matter will be, but I'll know instinctively when I need to grab my pen and notebook, and sometimes the first sentence or two will be in my mind before I even get started.

I don't meditate before starting to write, and I don't feel like I'm in any kind of trance state. I don't "hear" a voice with my ears. Instead, thoughts and sentences just start coming to my mind, and I write them down verbatim. Sometimes the thoughts are coming so fast that it's hard for me to keep up with them; other times they're very measured and at a pace that's easy to transcribe. The name Inner Dictation makes sense, because it's like taking dictation from thoughts. Someone else is coming up with the words, and I'm just writing them down.

One of the most important factors for me is not to question the words at all. It took me quite a while to be comfortable with that because I'm such a perfectionist when it comes to writing. When I'm writing something from my conscious human mind, I'll go over it and over it, making little changes here and there until I've decided it's acceptable. If I start doing that during the process of Inner Dictation, the communication stops immediately.

One of the things that made it easy for me to quit trying to judge or evaluate what was coming through is that the material essentially is presented in final form and almost never needs any editing. All I can do is smile at that reality and allow the words to flow.

It's very important to stay in a peaceful state while the process is happening. There often are "real world" distractions of one kind or another, in addition to the thoughts of the human mind that are always bouncing in and out, and I've become pretty good at simply ignoring them. If I allow myself to focus on them and become distracted, the communication usually stops, just as it does if I start to question the wording or the concepts.

It usually is clear when the communication is over, though there sometimes are natural pauses in the flow of thoughts that give me time to stretch or move about. When those little breaks are over, the communication almost always picks up exactly where it had left off before.

## How Source Describes It

The words above represent my human mind's best attempt to describe the experience for you, but occasionally over the years Source has talked about the process in the writings I've transcribed, presumably in an attempt to help me understand it better. I've pulled out some of those excerpts and am eager to share them with you.

### What it Feels Like

There really is an almost physical feeling to this form of communication, but it's hard for me to come up with words to describe it. Source, on the other hand, does not have that problem.

*Enjoy the fact that your hands once again are flying across the page with virtually no conscious thought on your part. You truly are in the flow, and you are allowing it to guide you. Feel the peace and the smoothness of it. Allow its simplicity to delight you.*

∞

*Remind yourself how free and natural and perfect this means of communication is. There is no stress, no strain. You simply allow it to flow naturally, and your good and your guidance are there for you immediately.*

∞

*Feel the flow here. It is instant and abundant. You are effortlessly claiming and accepting your good. Remember the feeling – it is one of complete trust, without any doubt or attempt to control. You are doing it now.*

∞

*It is beyond trust; it is simply emptying the channels of your mind of all of the accumulated garbage and allowing the words to flow.*

∞

*You know how effortless it is. It is always there, and only you can turn it off. Delight in it. Luxuriate in it. Allow it. Simply trust and allow. Accept and allow.*

∞

*Remember this feeling. Remember how you are simply allowing the words to flow. You are not judging them or weighing them or questioning them. You are claiming them and accepting them without resistance.*

## Why Staying in the Flow is Important

You probably noticed how often the word "flow" appeared in the segments above, and if you've read *Lessons from the Source* you know how beautifully the concept of flow is presented there. I've come to believe that to allow the words to flow through me without resistance while I'm writing them is to experience what it's like to be truly in the flow.

*Experience the flow, for you are in it. This is not a different flow simply for writing my words. This is the flow of goodness, and you are in it. Rejoice. Give thanks. Feel what it feels like. Accept it. Allow the restrictions to which you have given power to float away. Release them. Cut them loose. You are home again.*

∞

*Think of the flow. See it and feel it. Know that you are part of it. Focus on it and accept it. Rejoice in it. Maintain your awareness of it. Your ability to hear my words so clearly and to put them on the page so quickly is a physical manifestation of the flow. Remind yourself during the day how clear it was that you were here – and then know that you still are.*

*Allow the strength, yet gentleness, of the flow itself to wash away the remnants of your negative thinking. As you release them and let them go, give them a blessing and give thanks for the learning that you have experienced as a result of them. Then surrender to the goodness all around you. Accept it and claim it and rejoice in it. It is yours, and it is my desire that you have it and experience it and grow from it.*

∞

*Do not resist the flow of your good in any way. Do not create any obstacles to it. Simply be. Just as you are now. You are in a completely open, peaceful and accepting frame of mind. You are allowing my words to flow so smoothly that nothing interrupts them. This is how it should be. Feel for a moment what it feels like. Feel its smoothness and ease. Be aware that you have removed all examples of mental resistance to the flow. Your conscious mind is active only as a receptor for the good emanating from the God mind within you. It has no other role and seeks none. It is passive and peaceful.*

## How to Resist the Urge to Question or Control the Words

The human mind always seems to want to be in charge. It feels a need to understand, to figure things out, and to make things work the way it thinks they should. That tendency can be one of the greatest obstacles to receiving and transcribing wisdom from Source.

Early on in my experience with this process, I sometimes would find myself thinking that a sentence didn't make sense, or wondering where a certain narrative was leading. Occasionally I even wondered whether my human mind was making the words up itself. That questioning or needing to figure things out inevitably stopped the process right in its tracks.

As I said before, Inner Dictation is all about trusting and allowing, and Source never has been reluctant to point out when my human mind is trying to have its way.

*You are finding yourself questioning specific words that you are writing this morning. This is a subtle form of resistance to your flow. Shake it off and let it go. Be in the flow and let the thoughts come to you unimpeded.*

∞

*Are you absorbing what you are hearing and writing? Rather than rejoicing, you are doubting. You are asking yourself what words will come to you next – as if you were in control of this.*

*You must surrender the thoughts of your conscious mind to the thoughts that come from me through you. This is just as you must surrender your "will," which is the product of your conscious mind, to mine if you are to realize the fulfillment of my plan of total goodness for you.*

∞

*You do not need to control the flow of words. Your role specifically is not to try to control, but simply to accept, to allow, to be an open and unimpeded channel through which they may flow. Remove the blockage you have created. Resist not. Let go of it all. Simply accept.*

∞

*There is no need to struggle with this process. Allow the flow. Allow your entire being to be at peace. You are a conduit and not an evaluator. Peace, acceptance, perfection.*

∞

*Your willingness to believe that all of this is real is crucial. Yes, it is coming through your mind, but you are opening yourself (and your mind) to my wisdom and guidance. Do not pass judgment on what you are receiving. Simply put it on the page. As you have seen, the flow becomes natural and easy, and the lessons are coherent. You have done this for long enough that you must trust.*

There are occasions when the first words or sentences I receive seem absurd, and I'll be tempted to stop and start over again, but if I continue and allow the words to flow, the results almost always are magical. One example is the excerpt that I titled "Cooking up Creativity" in my previous e-book, *More Lessons from the Source*; and I'm including another in the Appendix at the end of this document.

### What to Do When Distractions Come Up
Sights or sounds or people – or the thoughts of your mind – can distract your attention from the flow of wisdom from Source, and

those distractions can be another way to bring the process to a quick halt. It's important to learn to simply ignore them.

> *There are so many distractions around you. The sounds from the street have stopped the flow of my words to you. You will learn, as you continue this process, to allow those things which you now consider to be distractions to enhance the process, for you will understand that all that you can hear or see or feel or smell are simply manifestations of my presence, and this realization will reinforce the experience you are having.*

∞

> *The noise you have been hearing while writing this is an illustration of the importance of silence in your life, and silence is another essential pathway to peace. Just as you give power to other types of conditions, you also give power to sounds that distract you and keep your mind from opening itself to your ultimate reality. Discipline is so important to your growth, and you must be rigorous in your practice of it.*

∞

> *Let go of the internal chatter and quiet your mind. When your mind is at peace, these words can flow freely to you. But your mind must be still. You have begun to become aware of the ways in which it interferes with the flow. When you do, simply direct it to be at peace and to open itself to the flow of goodness.*

∞

> *Thoughts about the issues you are facing during your day-to-day "reality" in the physical world have easy access to your mind, and as soon as they enter, you allow your access to my wisdom and guidance to be restricted. They are still flowing to you and available to you in every instance, yet it still is a challenge to you to keep the channel open and unimpeded.*

# A Broader Perspective on All This

Because this communication with Source has been such an important part of my life for so many years, I've come to see it not simply as an interesting phenomenon that has changed my life, but also as part of a bigger picture that I believe has meaning and implications for all of us.

## We All Are Creative

I'm fascinated by the concept of creativity and its infinite expressions.

I like to think of creativity as a process through which an individual human being allows something that never before has existed in physical form to come through him or her into the physical world.

We often tend to define creativity in terms of art or music or design or writing, but it could be almost anything – including the kind of communication I've been describing to you. Is there really any difference between a songwriter composing a new tune, or an architect designing a new building, or a software engineer building a new application for your phone, or my receiving and writing down a new interpretation of spiritual truth?

It seems to me the key factor in any form of creativity is our willingness and ability to *allow* whatever it is that is longing to emerge into physical form to happen through us. And when we are able to allow, we become co-creators with the Source of all goodness.

I found this little paragraph among the writings:

*You are a co-creator with me. This writing is a perfect example of that. The words are mine, but you must transcribe them. Your mind and your hands are the channel. There are so many ways in which you can (and do!) serve as a channel for my good and co-create wonders on the earth plane.*

What does creativity look like to you? How do you co-create with God?

It's possible that you've also been given the gift of being able to access wisdom from the Source. And if you have, the end product could be something very different from what I receive.

But if you haven't, so what? Your gift might very well be something that expresses itself in an entirely different way and affects the world by touching exactly the people who need it at precisely the right moment in their lives.

We all are able to be co-creators. The key is being willing and able to allow.

## We All Have Access to Guidance

I've been thinking lately about this statement in the section on Guidance in *Lessons from the Source*:

> *There is always help available to you. It is there for you in forms that you cannot yet imagine or remember because of the limitations of human consciousness, but it is unfailingly there. You must let go and trust.*

The voice speaking through the writings makes it very clear that the Inner Dictation I experience is only one of those many forms of guidance that are always available to me, and when I forget about that, it is never reluctant to remind me:

> *You are learning to accept my word when you are writing, and you must learn to do the same when you are not.*
>
> *At times, you feel that you are unsuccessful in hearing my guidance. And yet you write out my words each day and accept them as truth. Know that, just as I am here when you take your pen in your hand, I am also here at any time of need in your life. My wisdom is always available to you. You need only make yourself available to it. Trust that the answers are there for you at any moment. They do not need to come to you through meditation or through a dream or any other specific method. Simply ask (which is what you are doing when you sit down to write and expect my words to be there), and it will be given to you. You will be able to put yourself in the flow of my truth just as easily at any time of need as you do when you write.*
>
> *It is interesting, isn't it, that you are much more willing to accept the reality of our communication when it relates to deep spiritual truths than when it concerns specific decisions in your day-to-day life on earth. Which is more important or of greater magnitude? If you can trust on the grand scale, how much more logical is it to trust on the mundane level?*

What an important reminder! Just like creativity, I believe we all have access to God's guidance, and there's no one way (and certainly no right or wrong way) to get it. Again, it's about being open and available and willing to allow.

## We All Can Manifest Our Good Without Struggle

One of my greatest struggles in life has always been manifesting my desires – bringing into my life the things and conditions that I believe are for my highest good. I understand the spiritual principles of manifestation and can preach them as well as the next guy, but something in me always seems to be resisting my good or blocking it in some way. Often, I've felt that I've needed to find a way to make it happen by myself, rather than simply asking and trusting and allowing. (There's that word again.)

Fortunately, that has begun to change, and I believe it is happening in part because of a number of reminders from Source that I already have the prototype for doing so. Here's a good example. Check it out.

> *You can literally feel yourself allowing these words of truth and counsel to flow to you and through you onto the page. This is a very important, and easily accepted, reminder of the ease and effortlessness with which your good can be claimed and accepted.*
>
> *Free access. Think about that. Free can and does imply "unlimited" or "unimpeded," but it also is "free" in the most simple sense of the word – without "cost." But it is not without commitment. Here is the truth you need in this moment, coming to you in abundant measure from the greatest authority anyone could imagine, without any consulting fee or obligation. But the commitment to truly put these truths into practice in your life and to live them is your responsibility.*
>
> *The words are continuing to flow to you without pause or effort. They are exactly what you need. The other forms of goodness you desire are just as easy to claim and accept, but the fact that they affect the "quality" of your life in the physical world that you have been trained so assiduously to believe is full of restrictions and limitations makes them seem more difficult to bring forth into manifestation.*
>
> *But there is no difference – none at all. Think of how your day-to-day existence would, and can, be different and so much richer, if you simply (again, a reminder of the true simplicity of it all – as if this experience of flow were not sufficient) claimed and accepted them as*

*effortlessly as you are claiming and accepting this communication by sitting in a comfortable chair with a cup of coffee and with pen and paper.*

*There is no difference in your ability to access the blessings that would enhance your life in the ways you desire. This very same phenomenon can and should be used and called on and accepted with regard to the blessings you desire and feel sorely missing in your daily life.*

*You are pleasantly surprised at how this communication is still flowing so effortlessly after such a long session. You are simply reminding yourself of how effortless and easily accessible it is. You are allowing. Your conscious mind is offering no doubts or objections or impediments. It simply is allowing the blessings to flow.*

*Know in the deepest recesses of your being that this same access is always, always available to you concerning any desire of your heart, for those desires are my desires for you. Your good in the form of financial supply or creativity or professional opportunities is just as easily accessible.*

*There for a fleeting moment your human mind began to object by attempting to show a difference between this communication which is "ethereal" (the word that came to you) and the manifestation of those other blessings which will show up in physical form. But how much more physical can you get than these words on a piece of paper that you and the entire world can see?*

*Much of one's financial supply is never even seen. The dollars that you carry with you and exchange with others are only a small percentage of the number of dollars you receive and circulate in the world. The vast majority of that "physical" supply is never seen, but is circulated freely and accepted by others without any doubt or reservation.*

*So the case has been made, irrefutably, to your now-struggling conscious mind that its objection has no merit. And that, in turn, allows you to dismiss it immediately.*

*There is no difference between your ability to claim and accept this communication and the other forms of goodness you desire. None whatsoever. Let go of the struggle, for it is a product of the conflict between your human mind and the truth that overrides it. Accept that reality and allow this same flow that is so freely and effortlessly allowing you to communicate in this way to bring the other blessings you desire into manifestation.*

That type of reminder has helped me begin to let go of the need to make things happen on my own and to live from a perspective of trust, acceptance and allowing.

It has taken a long time for me to allow the concepts that have been presented over and over again to sink in and truly change my life – but it has happened, and the gradual transformation continues.

I remember realizing a number of years ago that the negative emotions that had been so very present in my consciousness during most of my life essentially were gone. Fear, worry, stress, anger, judgment – daily emotions that I almost took for granted – now seldom show up in my mind. I still smile to myself that the change had happened so gradually that I wasn't even consciously aware of it, but it has happened, and it's very liberating not to have to deal with that negativity on a daily basis.

Letting go of my human mind's need to be in control and make things happen is taking longer, and it certainly is not gone completely, but that evolution is happening, and I'm very grateful for it.

# What About You?

I'll be curious to learn how this e-book has touched your life.

- Perhaps it will resonate and offer a new perspective for those of you who have had similar experiences with receiving messages from somewhere other than your conscious human mind.

- If this whole concept of channeling wisdom is new to you, as it was to me, I trust that it will have made you more open to the possibility.

- But I'm especially hoping it will inspire some of you – including those for whom journaling is a regular practice – to explore the possibility of opening yourselves to this type of communication, or something like it.

If you're intrigued by what you've read here and feel inclined to explore this form of channeling on your own, I encourage you to give it a try – but without any specific expectations.

I certainly can't guarantee that you'll experience anything like what I've described, but if you can get out of the way and open yourself to the flow and allow whatever might be waiting to flow through you to do so, my guess is that you'll be in for some pleasant surprises.

We all have different gifts, and I believe creativity flows through each of us as channels using the intrinsic talents we brought into the world with us. You might not experience Inner Dictation, but you could find yourself being guided to allow something entirely different to be brought forth into the world. Be open to whatever presents itself.

# Some Suggestions for You

I'm confident that some of you will have been sufficiently intrigued by what you've read here to want to see what might happen if you were to open yourself to this form of communication. If that's the case, here are a few suggestions for you, based on my experience:

1) **Find a quiet, peaceful place to open yourself to the flow.** I have a specific spot in my home where I go to write when I feel moved to do so, but I've been able to receive the communications in lots of different environments – some of which don't seem very peaceful at all. I've found my receptivity to be especially enhanced when I'm in a beautiful outdoor setting. You might find it in a formal garden like the Lake Shrine, a path through a forest, a mountaintop, a river or stream...or your own back yard. The specific location doesn't matter as long as you feel open and receptive.

2) **Don't try to force anything to happen.** If nothing comes to your mind right away, that's OK. I've sometimes found that, when I feel eager to receive something immediately, it simply isn't there. The timing of all this, after all, is not ours to determine.

As I mentioned, I'll often have an inner knowing (almost an urging) that it's time to start writing, but there's a qualitative difference between that inner nudging and my own mind's deciding that it's ready to communicate. I'm confident you'll be able to tell the difference.

By the same token, if you feel a calling to sit down and write, and the words don't begin to flow, just be patient and trust. Try to keep your mind as still and as empty as possible and begin writing only when a thought that feels like it's coming from somewhere other than your own conscious mind pops into your head.

(By the way, you might find yourself more receptive when sitting at your computer or tablet than with a pen and paper in your hand, and that's perfectly OK. I'm from a generation that grew into adulthood long before computers were part of everyday life, and writing the messages longhand is easier and more comfortable for me, but I can't believe Source has any preferences about how we transcribe its words.)

3) **Be open and available to whatever it is that might be waiting for you.** Your experience with Inner Dictation could be different from mine – or you

might find yourself experiencing some other form of channeling or creativity. Maybe you *will* hear a voice, as opposed to receiving thoughts; or you could experience automatic writing, where your hand would be moving of its own volition. Or, depending on what Source might be communicating through you, you could begin writing a novel, or understanding a design concept, or hearing a tune that has never been heard before, or getting an idea for a work of art.

**4) When/if the words or concepts begin to flow, simply accept them without any resistance or distractions.** Again, don't try to force anything or to be in control. Regardless of what you might be receiving, the most important factor from my perspective is being able to get your human mind out of the way and then to trust and allow the flow to move through you without any interruptions.

Interruptions or distractions can come in many different ways, but most of them will be from your own mind. Extraneous thoughts about things going on in your life can distract you from the process. If you try to figure out what might be coming next or how you could improve or enhance the wording, the flow of words is likely to stop. Learning to ignore, and then let go of, those pesky interruptions might take a while, but it's essential to mastering the process.

**5) Don't be concerned about where the information is coming from.** While you might never know for sure, there almost always will be indicators of one kind or another.

The teachings I've been blessed to receive over the years have been in a consistent voice that is always gentle, loving, supportive, encouraging and non-judgmental. That says to me that the origin of the material is benevolent, kind and good, and the fact that the material comes through in final form and seldom needs editing is all the evidence I need that it's not from my conscious human mind.

I've heard of instances where people have channeled voices that are harsh, negative or critical. There's no telling where they might be coming from – possibly from that person's own mind or from some entity that was less than loving – but if that were to happen to me, I almost certainly would stop immediately.

As I explained in *Lessons from the Source*, the voice speaking through the material I receive has never specifically identified itself, but the very clear implication is that it is God, or Source, or whatever other term you might consider appropriate.

But of course people receive channeled communication from a seemingly limitless number of entities that do identify themselves. The voice speaking through *A Course in Miracles* (the best known example of Inner Dictation) is said to be Jesus; Esther Hicks channels a group of entities who call themselves Abraham; Jane Roberts received communications from Seth; JZ Knight channels Ramtha, etc.

To my mind, the identification of the source of the communication is far less important than the information or teachings being conveyed.

I've often used an analogy comparing spiritual truth to a huge diamond with an infinite number of facets. As you examine the diamond through different facets, you get a slightly different perspective on it, but it still is a diamond.

I believe there can be an infinite number of interpretations of spiritual truth coming through channels or teachers or books or religions – all offering slightly different perspectives on life and spirituality; and each of those interpretations will resonate with certain individuals.

If you begin receiving information from somewhere other than your own human mind, the source of that information might or might not identify itself, but I don't believe that really matters. If the nature of the material that is being conveyed through you is helpful and meaningful, I would encourage you not to be overly concerned with knowing exactly where it came from.

# Conclusion

I trust that what you've read here has been informative and intriguing and has offered a helpful perspective on the connection I believe we all have to Source. If you've been inspired to explore your own connection and ways in which it might express through you, I would love to hear from you about your experiences.

But my greatest hope is that you will begin thinking about creativity and guidance and access to your higher good from a different vantage point. However we interpret them, all of those are available to each of us in every moment of our journey – if we can simply allow.

Much love and many blessings to you.

# Appendix A: My Spiritual Quest

I'm very aware that what I've shared with you in this e-book is not about me, yet many of you have asked about my own spiritual journey. While I don't consider it to be any more remarkable than anyone else's (after all, we all travel our own unique paths), it does occur to me that knowing a little about how my spiritual life has evolved might offer a helpful context for what you've read about my role in the process. So here's a brief summary.

When I was growing up, our family was very active in a mainstream Protestant denomination, and we went to church every Sunday. I didn't object to that – it's just what we did. I received a good grounding in a Christian spirituality that was not overly dogmatic, but what I was taught never really grabbed me or felt so convincing that it I thought it ought to be the foundation for the way I lived the rest of my life.

But that introduction to the spiritual side of life clearly must have sparked something in me, because I always seemed to be looking for a bigger perspective on it all. I think I was hoping to find a belief system that would feel comfortable for me – not one that simply had been passed along and that I would be expected to accept without questioning.

My first memory of searching for something different was seeing an advertisement for the Rosicrucian Fellowship while I was in high school and sending away for information. It promised to offer a new perspective, and I found that intriguing.

As a college student, I was exposed to interpretations of life and spirituality that were entirely new to me, and thinking about them made the Christian principles I had been taught seem rather limited – not inaccurate or inappropriate, but limited.

After college I served in the Peace Corps in Uruguay, a country where organized religion played only a minimal role. Yet most of the Uruguayans I knew and worked with were good, kind, generous people who seemed to be living life joyously and peacefully without following a specific set of religious beliefs, and that, too, offered food for thought.

After the Peace Corps, my searching continued, and it's never really stopped. Here, in roughly chronological order, are some of the experiences I've had along the way that have helped to broaden my perspective:

Dabbled briefly in Catholicism at a church offering contemporary folk masses for young people.

Attended a Unitarian church where I inevitably would leave feeling joyous and glad to be alive. (Unfortunately I made the mistake of telling my mom in a letter what a wonderful experience it was, and she wrote back telling me how disappointed she was that I had been attending a church that didn't "believe in God.")

Worked together with a group of friends in organizing a progressive Protestant church with a style of worship and an interpretation of Christianity we all could feel comfortable with. That noble effort fell apart after the minister we hired became involved in an affair with one of the members.

Spent a good bit of time investigating Spiritualism, which involves communication between the physical and spiritual worlds through mediums. While living in Florida I made frequent visits to a spiritualist colony called Cassadaga, and during our time in Washington, DC, we attended the Church of Two Worlds. I still use some of the affirmations I picked up during that time.

Explored my own abilities as a healer. I read books about hands-on healing and had many experiences where I was able to relieve other people's physical pain. They often commented about how hot my hands felt.

Subscribed to Unity's *Daily Word* decades ago and attended a number of different Unity and Religious Science (as it was known then) churches over the years.

Joined, enjoyed, was nurtured by, and served on the Board of Directors of an independent New Thought church in California. The minister became a spiritual mentor and mother figure to me, and she and I remained close until her death in 2012. After she retired, the experience was never the same. I left the church and haven't belonged to another one since.

Attended Rev. Michael Beckwith's Agape International Spiritual Center in Los Angeles for a number of years and was awed and inspired by his presence.

I guess I'm not a very churchy guy. From time to time since moving to the Northwest, I've visited different churches and tried them out, but none has felt like home. If a worship experience feels comforting and nurturing and joyous, I love it and will keep coming back for more. I like to sit quietly and feel the peace, and I actually enjoy singing the old church hymns from my youth. But worship styles have changed, and the more contemporary formats often leave me cold.

It also sometimes seems to me that much of the focus of church services is on the church itself, as an entity or an institution. For a while many years ago, I attended a New Thought church almost every week and found the nourishment and peace I desired during the services, but had no interest at all in the pot luck dinners or fundraisers or committees. One Sunday the minister essentially said during her sermon that, if someone was just coming to church on Sunday and not becoming part of the community, they probably need not be there. I never went back.

# Appendix B: Peanut Butter

In describing the process of Inner Dictation, I mentioned the need for the human mind to step out of the way and allow whatever is presented to be transcribed onto the page without any questions or judgments. The following passage, which I received on October 22, 2008, was one of the greatest tests of my ability/willingness to do that.

The first words that came through were "peanut butter." While it seemed highly unlikely that this truly was Source speaking, I took a leap of faith and wrote the words down and kept on going, and I've always been glad I did. Here is the complete writing from that day.

> *Peanut butter.*
>
> *You did it. You were willing to take a term that you were sure had been concocted by your human mind and put it on the page out of trust, though you had no idea at all what it meant or why you were asked to write it.*
>
> *Peanut butter is of a very thick consistency. It originates from individual nuts that had been taken from shells, that had been taken from a plant, that had arisen seemingly from nowhere because someone had planted a seed and trusted, while doing all that he or she knew to nurture its development and evolution and transformation into a plant.*
>
> *Once the plant appeared (again seemingly out of nowhere), a human continued to nurture it and take steps to allow it to develop and grow and flourish so that its role in the world (to produce the peanuts, carefully encased and protected by a tough outer shell) could be fulfilled. That process of evolution took place without the human's need to control or direct. His or her responsibility was to nurture – and then to trust that the shell would appear (yes, seemingly from nowhere) and that the peanuts would develop perfectly, outside of the sight of the human.*
>
> *At the appropriate time (which the human understood instinctively, because there was no visible evidence of the perfection of the individual peanuts), the shells were picked out of complete trust – virtual certainty, in fact – that the peanuts would be perfectly developed inside of the shells. There was no doubt or worry or fear about them being there or being perfect – it was a certainty accepted without question. Yes, there would be individual shells with individual peanuts that might not meet the human's expectations or understanding of perfection, but the vast,*

*enormous majority of them were seen as perfect. (Of course the human's expectations and understanding were limited in their ultimate scope.)*

*Effortless perfection. The plant did not struggle, it allowed. The human did not worry, it trusted.*

*Now let's get back to our original topic of peanut butter. This is where the effort of the human consciousness, directed by its higher consciousness, comes into play. Another type of transformation is required. Specific actions are necessary on the human plane to transform the peanuts, which appeared seemingly from nowhere in effortless perfection, into peanut butter.*

*It just occurred to you that the peanuts in either form (individual nuts or butter) can be eaten and enjoyed by humans and offer nourishment to them. So the needs (food for sustenance) and desires (an appealing taste) of the humans are met by a human's complete trust and acceptance and allowing (while taking action on his or her part to nurture) on the one hand, totally accepting effortless perfection, and then his or her following the guidance that he or she receives directly and intuitively (or that someone else had received and passed along for the benefit of others) and taking the necessary action on the human plane to facilitate the transformation from nuts to butter.*

*So, you see, this is but one of an infinite and ever-growing number of examples of human trust and acceptance and allowing of effortless perfection – the creation of something in the physical world that appeared from seeming nothingness – followed by specific action, again trusting in guidance from the unseen, to take the new entity and transform it into something that will meet the needs and aspirations of that individual human, or some specific constituency, or of all humanity.*

*There is a difference between control and nurturance. In both cases, specific actions are necessary on your part, but there is a fine line in the human mind between demanding perfection and allowing it.*

*The person who "invented" peanut butter did not know specifically what would result from taking the actions he or she was being guided to take, for the "reality" of peanut butter itself did not yet exist. It was a question of taking the fruits of effortless perfection and trusting in the guidance and direction without having any real idea of what the specific outcome would be. And that person's willingness to trust without needing to control resulted in a food substance that has delighted untold millions of people – and continues to do so.*

*Of course, over time other individuals have improved upon that original substance by following their intuitive, creative sense of how it might be adapted to create even greater pleasure for the people who consume it – and to create greater financial abundance for themselves, for both peanut butter and money are examples of my substance at work in the world.*

I still am in awe when I read that passage and am delighted that I didn't give up on it.

You probably noticed the frequent use of the term "effortless perfection." That concept is one that has been presented and explained in the writings frequently over the years, and I look forward to sharing some of those writings with you in the future.

# Other Books by Jack Armstrong:

*Lessons from the Source:*
*A Spiritual Guidebook for Navigating Life's Journey*

*More Lessons from the Source:*
*Practical Wisdom for Enjoying Life's Journey*

*You Don't Need to Conduct the Orchestra:*
*Lessons on Letting Go, Trusting and Allowing*

Life's journey is one we all share and navigate together. We are never alone. To get more information, find other products and services by Jack Armstrong, and join a growing online community of loving adventurers sharing experiences and finding the joy in their journey, please visit:

**www.lessonsfromthesource.com**

www.ingramcontent.com/pod-product-compliance
Lightning Source LLC
Chambersburg PA
CBHW071748020426
42331CB00008B/2221